IS ANYBODY
OUT THERE?

JOHN BLANCHARD

EVANGELICAL PRESS

EVANGELICAL PRESS
Faverdale North, Darlington, DL3 0PH, England

e-mail: sales@evangelicalpress.org

Evangelical Press USA
P. O. Box 825, Webster, New York 14580, USA

e-mail: usa.sales@evangelicalpress.org

web: http://www.evangelicalpress.org

First published 2006

British Library Cataloguing in Publication Data available

ISBN-13   978-0-85234-616-7   ISBN 0-85234-616-6

Printed and bound in the United Kingdom by Graham & Heslip, Belfast.

For nearly half a century a privately funded project has captured the imagination of millions of people all around the world. SETI (Search for Extraterrestrial Intelligence) was launched in the hope of stumbling across messages from alien civilization in outer space, but it ties in with deeper questions that human beings have been asking for thousands of years. Are we alone in the universe? Are we the most intelligent creatures in existence? Is there a cosmic life force? If there is, can we get in touch with it?

Frank Drake, the American astronomer who launched SETI in 1960, gave it an added dimension and said that the project was really a search for ourselves — who we are and where we fit into the cosmic scheme of things. Yet for countless people, the search points to an even more fundamental question: *Does God exist?*

Some ask the question out of scientific or philosophical interest, or merely out of curiosity. Others ask it only when the news media report a major catastrophe, or when they themselves are gripped by pain, insecurity, depression or despair. Whatever the trigger, it is no exaggeration to say that every question about human life or death, or about the universe in which we are living and dying, ultimately revolves around it.

Is anybody out there? *We need to know.*

The faith factor

For many people, discussing the existence of God raises a question that ultimately relates to every issue we could ever debate: *Why should anyone believe anything at all?* This seems a perfectly reasonable question, but it self-destructs, because even to believe that one has no need to believe anything is in itself believing something. This points to the fact that believing is one of the characteristics that define us as human beings. We seem inescapably programmed to believe things. Believing is as natural as breathing, an automatic function that only attracts our attention when we stop to think about it. We can no more opt out of believing than we can shrug off our own skins. Believing — that is, having faith — is not an option. Even to say that it is an option is to express a statement of faith.

It is no exaggeration to say that we live by faith, in that it influences every part of our lives. Whenever we make a decision about anything, even the smallest, everyday things, we believe not only that we have valid reasons for doing so, but that we are qualified to say that such reasons are valid. Relying on reason is itself an act of faith.

At a practical level, we trust that our senses are

reliable and that we are therefore right to believe what they tell us. Even when they register things that are invisible, such as sound or smell, we believe that our ears and noses are registering reality and not fantasy. This underlines the fact that every part of our lives is tied in to our beliefs. Even when we change our minds, faith is the determining factor. We begin by believing something, then we believe we are mistaken, then we believe something different — and at every stage faith calls the tune. Without faith it would be impossible for us to live and function in a meaningful way and as what we believe radically affects how we behave, faith is the engine driving all our actions. Without it, we would be utterly paralysed.

Fundamental questions such as 'Who am I?', 'Why am I here?' and 'Where am I going?' have generated a vast variety of answers. Yet here, too, the answers are matters of faith, based on reasons that may be coloured by a person's upbringing or culture, or based on religious teaching of some kind. People believe in all sorts of ideas: about their origin and destiny, the meaning and purpose of life, their place in the cosmos, the problem of pain, the approach of death and the existence or otherwise of the afterlife. Most people have beliefs about all of these — *and no one has no beliefs about any of them.* Over 2,300 years ago the Greek philosopher Aristotle wrote, 'All men by nature desire to know.' He was right. We are incurably inquisitive and every discovery we make adds to the structure of what we believe.

The faith factor is just as dominant when we consider the question of God's existence, in that there are no 'non-believers'. The atheist claims God does not exist; the agnostic says God may or may not exist; the theist is convinced God does exist — but all are believers, convinced that their position can be validly held. On this and on every other issue it is literally impossible to believe nothing at all.

This raises the ultimate and inescapable question: *Why believe in God?*

The blind alley

Opinion polls on everything from politics to pop stars often have a box labelled 'Don't know'. This can be used to register genuine uncertainty, but it can also be treated as an escape hatch to avoid commitment one way or the other. Those who tick the 'Don't know' box in answer to the question 'Does God exist?' are known as *agnostics,* and many who do this feel that they have successfully dodged the question. But have they?

Agnostics come in two brands. The *soft-core agnostic* says, 'I don't know whether God exists' and often feels that he or she has neatly wriggled out of opting for anything. But because the issue is so serious this approach is hardly sensible. The question of God's existence is unlike any other. For example, theories about the existence of the Loch Ness Monster have been circulating for over 1,300 years, but in spite of all the reported sightings and grainy photographs I remain an agnostic about the existence of the beast. Fortunately, my agnosticism has no relevance to my life or lifestyle, my death, or what happens to me after I die. The question of God's existence, on the other hand, is dynamically related to all of these. That being so, does it make sense to slip into the 'Don't know' box and leave it at that? Is it wise to leave such vital questions about life, death and eternity hanging in the air?

The British industrialist Cecil Rhodes, who was powerfully influential in the development of South Africa and Zimbabwe (then named Rhodesia in his honour), once said, 'I've considered the existence of God and decided there's a 50-50 chance that God exists, and therefore I propose to give him the benefit of the doubt.' The soft-core agnostic may agree with Rhodes on the odds for or against God's existence, but then opts to give the benefit of the doubt to his doubts. As countless millions of people since time began have testified to the transforming power of God in their lives, surely this is a wishy-washy kind of response? Would it not show more spine — and more sense — to examine the evidence and see where it leads? Is it wise to wait until all your questions are answered before committing yourself?

The *hard-core agnostic* goes much further than his soft-core cousin and claims it is impossible for *anyone* to know whether God exists. This seems to show more conviction but it can never get to its feet. The hard-core agnostic says that on the question of God's existence the only knowable truth is that there is no such thing as knowable truth — in other words, that there can be no agnosticism about agnosticism. Does this make sense?

Far from being reasonable, this kind of agnosticism turns out to be exactly the opposite. If you are reading this as a hard-core agnostic, how can you say that it is impossible to know whether God exists unless you know everything it is possible to know? It is easy to see that when we examine it closely hard-core agnosticism is self-defeating because it assumes knowledge of ultimate truth in order to deny that knowledge of ultimate truth is possible. It may sound like a comfortable option, but it leads nowhere. It is a blind alley.

The desert

The *Oxford Dictionary of English* defines atheism as 'the theory or belief that God does not exist', and the French philosopher Etienne Borne fleshes this out as follows: 'Atheism is the deliberate, definite, dogmatic denial of the existence of God... It is not satisfied with approximate or relative truth, but claims to see the ins and outs of the game quite clearly — being the absolute denial of the Absolute.'

Yet not even this dogmatic assertion can disguise the fact that atheism is not a statement of undeniable truth, but simply a belief system — and one that in the absence of evidence calls for a gigantic leap of faith. What is more, when atheism is closely examined, then pressed to its logical conclusion, it clearly fails to live up to its extravagant claims. It is like a vast desert, a bleak and barren landscape with no life-giving water to be found anywhere. Here are some examples of the way in which atheism comes up empty:

• It offers no coherent commentary on the existence of the universe. Instead, it settles for the British philosopher Bertrand Russell's view that 'The world is simply there and has no explanation.' This kills off any discussion, but hardly satisfies the serious thinker.

• It can supply no reason for the universe or for anything that lives or happens in it. It tells us nothing about the origin of life, whether in plants, animals or humans, and is forced to hide behind the idea that life is an accident of nature.

• It cannot point to any meaning for life. The well-known British atheist Peter Atkins says, 'We're just a bit of slime on a planet', but can we seriously live as if this were the case? If life is just the chance result of impersonal forces we find ourselves stranded in an absurd and meaningless world, with no basis for significance or hope.

• It provides no solid foundation for logical thinking and reduces the laws of logic to personal opinion or to uncertain principles that, like goods and services, are 'subject to change without notice'. But this is like building a castle on a quagmire and can hardly be used as an effective tool to dismiss the existence of God. To change the metaphor, atheism leans heavily on logic, but then kicks down the wall that is holding it up.

• It can give us no secure basis for objective and stable moral values, yet without these there can be no way of knowing the difference between right and wrong, or of knowing for certain how to react to situations that demand a moral response.

• It can bring no comfort to the homeless, the refugee, the starving, the hurting or the traumatized. To accept with the French atheist Jacques Monod that we are 'alone in the unfeeling vastness of the universe' is to make a nonsense of human relationships.

• Denying God's existence provides no guarantee that good will eventually triumph over evil.

• In the absence of a transcendent God there is no possibility of life after death.

We will refer to some of these in the following pages, but in the light of what they tell us are you happy to settle for a life controlled by this kind of thinking? The French philosopher Jean-Paul Sartre taught that man had been dumped into a meaningless universe and was caught between 'the absurdity of life's origin and the fear of life's extinction'. After fifty years spent developing a godless worldview he was forced to this telling conclusion: 'Atheism is a cruel, long-term business.'

The vacuum

The distinguished British scientist Sir John Houghton says, 'There is general evidence that most human beings, from whatever part of the world, and from the earliest times, have exhibited a fundamental belief in a divine being or beings.' This is backed up by the fact that *The Encyclopaedia of Religion and Ethics* runs to thirteen large volumes, giving details of a bewildering array of religious ideas about supernatural reality.

Of all the religious systems known to man, only four are commonly called 'world religions' in that they nominally claim five per cent or more of the world's population. These are Christianity (33%), Islam (21%), Hinduism (14%) and Buddhism (5%). Yet anybody searching for a personal religion has a staggering choice, taking in everything from astrology to alchemy, magic to macumba, pantheism to paganism and spiritism to satanism. Official figures published in 2004 said that in Britain alone there were nearly 200 different faiths or belief systems, including vodun (voodoo) and worship based around the peyote, a hallucinogenic cactus. In assessing the significance of this spiritual 'supermarket', four important things can be said.

Firstly, it points to the reality of the supernatural. The seventeenth-century French genius Blaise Pascal once famously wrote, 'There is a God-shaped vacuum in the heart of man and only God can fill it', while centuries later his fellow countryman, the influential thinker Jean-Paul Sartre, added his personal testimony: 'Everything in me calls for God and that I cannot forget.'

Secondly, sincerity about the truth of one's belief system is no guarantee of its integrity. Many a pilot or ship's captain sincerely believed he was on the right track only for his flight or voyage to end in disaster. Truth is objective, not subjective, and sincerity is no guarantee that a claim is valid.

Thirdly, in spite of enthusiastic efforts to bring different religions together in multi-faith movements and events, it is absurd to suggest that all religions are saying essentially the same thing. They may, of course, agree about *some* things: the four world religions commend honesty, humility and kindness, while condemning pride, greed, envy and selfishness. They may also agree on how to implement certain aspects of social policy: different religions can at times co-operate in seeking to counter serious problems in local or national society — and could even be joined by atheists. But a consensus on some points of morality cannot hide major differences in doctrine, especially those that relate to the existence, personality and attributes of a supreme God, the true significance of human life and the reality or otherwise of life beyond the grave. These are hardly trivial matters.

Fourthly, although all religions may theoretically be wrong, they cannot all be right, because each has beliefs that render those of others false. God cannot at one and the same time exist and not exist, nor can he be both personal and impersonal, remote and accessible. This makes it crystal clear that all religions *cannot* be the same if they are divided on the most important issues of all — the existence and nature of God.

But is there one that on the fundamental issues of reliability and truth stands apart from all the others? Is any one religion distinguished uniquely by the verifiable accuracy and unity of its foundational writings, the identity and perfection of its earthly founder, the integrity of its claims and the superiority of its moral influence? *There is.*

11

The truth

HOLY BIBLE

All major religions base their teaching on 'sacred' writing of some kind, but one text transcends all the others — the Bible. No other book has been so viciously attacked, with many of its translators imprisoned, tortured or murdered, and untold millions of copies destroyed. Yet it remains a global best-seller, now available in well over 2,000 language groups, covering over ninety per cent of the world's population. There are at least six clear reasons why this is the case.

Its text is more accurate than that of any other ancient book. Although copied by hand until the first printed version in 1455, its text has proved so amazingly consistent that Sir Frederic Kenyon, one-time director of the British Museum, concluded, 'The last foundation for any doubt that the Scriptures came down to us as they were written has finally been removed.'

Its history has proved impressively reliable. It records hundreds of national and international events, gives details about centuries of rulers and specifies the exact location of numerous towns and cities — and wherever its statements can be tested they have been found to be true. With over 25,000 sites now examined, Dr Nelson Glueck, the world's top biblical archaeologist, claims that 'no archaeological discovery has ever controverted a biblical reference'.

None of its scientific content has ever been proved wrong. While sometimes clashing with unproven theories, especially about origins, its statements on natural phenomena are completely in agreement with proven scientific facts. Sir Isaac Newton, universally recognized as one of the fathers of modern science, called the Bible 'a rock from which all the hammers of criticism have never chipped a single fragment'.

None of its prophecies has ever proved false. False prophets — and teachers who twist the truth to suit their own ends — are among the curses of religion, deluding and hurting many gullible people with their empty claims. Yet although some twenty-five per cent of the biblical text consists of history written in advance, none of these prophecies has proved false. Some 2,000 have already been fulfilled, giving good reason for believing that the rest will also prove true.

Its moral principles are without equal. No other literature can match its standards of truth, love, honesty or humility; its opposition to injustice, racism, oppression and greed; or its concern for the sick, the weak, the homeless, the poor and the dying. Many religions have become involved in commendable humanitarian projects, but the Bible's record as a motivating force for such is simply without parallel in human history.

Its teaching powerfully meets the deepest needs of human nature and experience. Its record of revolutionizing lives is unequalled and an untold number of people living today testify to its transforming influence. While not personally committed to its teaching, the eighteenth-century German thinker Immanuel Kant admitted, 'The existence of the Bible is the greatest blessing which humanity ever experienced.'

The Bible's unique integrity, authority and power ties in with its own claim that it is not a concoction of human ideas, but 'the living and enduring word of God'.[1] No other book claims this, yet the Bible does so from cover to cover. As it would be utterly illogical for the Bible to make blasphemous statements about its own authority yet be true on every other issue, we have good reason to trust everything it says. As the contemporary scholar R. C. Sproul puts it: 'If the Bible is trustworthy then we must take seriously the claim that it is more than trustworthy.'

This will be our approach from now on — beginning with its definition of God.

7 The ⁴law of the LORD perfect, ⁶converting the soul the ᵇtestimony of the LORD sure, making wise the simple. 8 The statutes of the LORD are right, rejoicing the heart: ᶜthe commandment of the LORD is pure, enlightening the eyes.
9 The fear of the LORD is clean, enduring for ever ⁱᵈgments of the

13

The LORD

When he was one of the famous Beatles in the 1960s, the British singer George Harrison said, 'When you use the word "God" people are going to curl up and cringe — they all interpret it in a different way.' He was right; on any given day, one can hear the word 'God' used to mean the object of a person's worship, some obscure cosmic force, a meaningless exclamation or a careless expletive. In stark contrast, the Bible says that any true knowledge of God is totally dependent on his revelation of himself. Of the many names and titles it uses of God to reflect different aspects of his nature, 'the LORD' appears well over 6,000 times and tells us that God is the sole and sovereign ruler of all other reality, past, present and future — 'the great King above all gods'.[2]

He was sovereign before time began. God is 'from everlasting to everlasting',[3] infinitely and eternally self-existent and unconstrained by time or space. As 'spirit'[4] he has no physical or material dimension. As 'the true God'[5] he reveals himself as a 'trinity' of three persons — the Father, the Son and the Holy Spirit — each of whom is truly, fully and equally God. As 'the eternal God'[6] his life is not a succession (not even an endless succession) of days, weeks, months and years. He neither ages nor tires and his plans 'stand firm for ever'.[7]

He is sovereign for all time. As 'Creator of heaven and earth'[8] he brought into being all reality outside of himself (time and space included) and now 'his kingdom rules over all'.[9] Yet although he is distinct from the entire universe, he is not an 'absentee landlord', but is everywhere present and active in it and 'works out everything in conformity with the purpose of his will'.[10] In doing so, he exercises all of his attributes, which include the following:

- God is all-powerful: 'The LORD does whatever pleases him.'[11]
- He is utterly holy: 'majestic in holiness, awesome in glory'.[12]
- He is perfectly just: 'righteousness and justice are the foundation of his throne'.[13]
- He is loving: 'his love endures for ever'.[14]

These alone (there are many others) are more than sufficient to dispel the common view of God as a vague celestial influence who can safely be ignored, or as a genial father-figure who is largely ignorant of what goes on and in any case has a relaxed attitude about our personal morality. Instead, they tell us that everything in our lives is 'uncovered and laid bare before the eyes of him to whom we must give account'.[15]

He will be sovereign after time ends. Many who deny God's existence claim to be happy with the idea that death is the end of human existence, but the Bible paints a very different picture. It rejects the idea of reincarnation by stating that 'man is destined to die once, and after that to face judgement'.[16] The Bible makes it crystal clear that human life has a moral dimension, that we are answerable every day to our Maker, and that after death 'each of us will give an account of himself to God'.[17] When that happens, God will 'judge the world with justice',[18] welcoming some into the fulness of 'eternal life' and condemning others to 'eternal punishment'.[19] Ignoring such a God is surely the height of human folly?

The beginning

Questions about origins have always fascinated us, from the time we first asked, 'Where do babies come from?' to the moment when we were first gripped by the cardinal question, 'Where did the universe come from?' Massive issues hinge on the answer, including who we truly are, how we got here and whether human life has any true significance or purpose. In the opening words of his celebrated television series *Cosmos* astrophysicist Carl Sagan announced, 'The cosmos is all that is, or ever was, or ever will be.' *But without knowing everything, how could anyone say this?*

Today's cosmologists have ditched the once-popular steady-state theory ('the universe had no beginning') and tell us that time and space did indeed have a beginning. Yet this still leaves the big question: how did it happen? The modern scholar Douglas Kelly pinpoints the options: 'Either one begins with faith in an eternal God or with faith in eternal matter. *There is nothing in between.*' But if we vote for eternal matter (or energy) how do we imagine it arranged itself in precisely the right complex order to create and sustain intelligent life on our planet? In *A Brief History of Time* the British astrophysicist Stephen Hawking pursues a 'Theory of Everything' that would tie all the cosmic conundrums together. Yet he eventually comes to this conclusion: 'Even if there is one possible unified theory, it is just a set of rules and equations. *What is it that breathes fire into the equations* and makes a universe for them to describe?'

Atheism says that in a sequence of events which nobody can prove, demonstrate or test, everything came from nothing, elegant laws of physics sprang from chaos, and life arose from non-life — eventually spawning intelligence, logic, self-consciousness, morality and our other defining features. This should be sufficient to tell us that the credibility of chance being the 'creator' lies in tatters. Giving chance a blank cheque produces questions, not answers; a bull in a china shop will not produce teapots. The order, harmony and complexity of the universe are clearly not self-generating, but cry out for a supernatural explanation. Intelligent Design (the idea dates back thousands of years) rightly argues that an intelligent cause is the best explanation for the ordered complexity we see in the natural world, but declines to go beyond the complexities themselves to find their explanation. The analytical philosopher Ludwig Wittgenstein had the wisdom to go further and say, 'The riddle of life in space and time lies outside space and time', while Isaac Newton declared that the universe's specified complexity 'could only proceed from the counsel and dominion of an intelligent and powerful Being'.

Modern science tells us that the universe has at least five essential elements — time, intelligence, energy, space and matter — and all are to be found in the Bible's opening sentence: 'In the beginning God created the heavens and the earth.'[20] 'In the beginning' speaks of time; 'God' speaks of intelligence; 'created' speaks of energy; 'the heavens' speaks of space; and 'the earth' speaks of matter. Is this nothing more than coincidence? C. S. Lewis said that he had never come across any philosophical theory about origins that was 'a radical improvement on these words'. They tell us that the secret of the universe lies not in some cosmological principle but in a transcendent person. As the Oxford don Keith Ward says, 'To grasp an idea of God is to grasp an idea of the only reality that could form a completely adequate explanation of the existence of the universe.' The order, consistency, harmony and beauty we see in the natural world reflect something of the glory of its Maker.

The 'assassin'

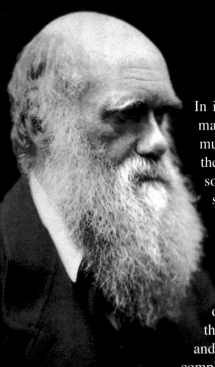

In its final issue of the twentieth century, *TIME* magazine said, 'Charles Darwin didn't want to murder God, but he did.' The 'bullet' used was the idea that beginning in some kind of primordial soup a simple form of life evolved by natural selection over millions of years into all living species, including humankind. Darwin's idea quickly became all the rage and within some fifty years the British biologist Sir Julian Huxley was calling it 'the most powerful and the most comprehensive idea that has ever arisen on earth'. Today, modern versions of Darwin's theory dominate Western thinking about the origin and development of life and for many people it completely disposes of God. But does it? Here are some of the facts that are at odds with the fanfare.

Nobody sensibly denies *microevolution* (changes within a given species or genus) but there is no solid evidence for *macroevolution* (changes linking all life forms). The British anatomist Sir Arthur Keith said this was 'unproved and unprovable' and frankly admitted, 'We believe it only because the alternative is special creation.' Macroevolutionism is not a science, but a belief system, with a prior commitment to naturalism (which rules out the supernatural or spiritual) regardless of its weaknesses. As naturalism is incapable of being tested by going back in time to recreate the radical changes it claims took place, it clearly fails to meet the scientific criteria it claims in its own support.

Naturalism has to invent its own starting point — one self-contained, self-replicating life form to get the whole evolution process started — but in trying to do so the best it can offer is guesswork. All attempts to generate life from inanimate elements have failed to produce even the simplest protein molecules on which life depends and no scientific journal has ever published a plausible explanation of how chemical evolution could have produced even the most basic molecular system, let alone a minnow, a mule or a man. Natural selection (the survival of the fittest) can be seen all around us, but never as the machinery that over millions of years could have turned nothing into nature, let alone protons into people. Nor does the fossil record produce evidence of gradual macroevolutionary development linking all known species. Colin Patterson, one-time senior palaeontologist at the British Museum, said that this institution contained 'not a particle of evidence' to support the idea.

Darwin said that if even one irreducibly complex system (one needing all of its interacting parts before it can function) existed that could not be formed by step-by-step evolution 'my theory would absolutely break down'. Yet we now know of many such systems that cannot be explained by any evolutionary process — including the eye's light sensory systems, the bacterial flagellum, the cilium, and the blood-clotting and immune system 'cascades'.

Naturalism cannot begin to explain why humans are so radically different from all other life forms, even those with similar DNA. Self-consciousness, a sense of personal dignity, aesthetic values, mathematical and linguistic skills, a moral dimension and concern about death and eternity find no explanation in naturalism — and if human life is the result of unplanned chemical evolution it is by definition meaningless. As the prominent British atheist Richard Dawkins admits, 'Natural selection, the blind, unconscious, automatic process which Darwin discovered, and which we now know is the explanation for the existence and apparently purposeful form of life, has no purpose in mind. It has no vision, no foresight, no sight at all.'

Macroevolution has been called 'the best idea anyone has ever had', but it remains nothing more than an idea. Darwin's 'bullet' does not even touch his target.

The Origin Of

MAN

19

The fingerprint

Nobody seriously denies that morality has profound and inescapable implications for human life. Not only do we face moral choices every day and know what it is to feel guilty or ashamed, we also find ourselves making moral judgements on whether other people's actions are right or wrong, good or bad, just or unjust, fair or unfair.

These choices and judgements make it impossible to escape the conclusion that as human beings *we are moral agents with moral obligations.* Whatever our personal standards we *know* that some things ought to be done while other things ought not to be done. This sense of obligation is imposed on us by our conscience, which overrides not only our social conditioning but our personal instincts and preferences. Brushing these aside, it commands us to do what we believe to be right and condemns us when we fail to toe the line. Everyone has a bad conscience about something, but where does conscience get this absolute moral authority?

Some people imagine that it comes from *nature*, but how can this be the case if the universe is no more than matter, energy, time and chance? How can the natural world hold us responsible for moral actions? We are all subject to the laws of physics, but we have no moral obligation to them. Even Richard Dawkins admits that as a basis for morality 'nature is not on our side'.

Others say that *personal judgement* is a sufficient basis for moral decisions and that, as philosopher Richard Rorty claims, 'There is nothing deep down inside us except what we have put there ourselves, no criterion that we have not created.' But this idea implodes as soon as we touch it. If individuals could choose their own rules social harmony would be impossible, as nobody would have the right to say that anyone else was wrong.

Social convention is an equally flimsy basis. How can we be sure that public opinion is any better than private opinion? Which convention shall we choose? What do we do when one culture clashes with another — or when cultures change? How can any given culture be a dependable basis for morality if it has no secure reference point of its own?

The failure of such things to provide a solid basis for moral values tells us that these values must be rooted in something other than human experience, interest or need. In the absence of absolute values there is no basis on which we can make moral judgements about anything or anyone. Conscience's authority demands a basis that is transcendent, perfect, unchanging and personal — *and God is all four*. He is above and beyond all other reality, 'exalted as head over all'.[21] We are specifically told that 'the law of the LORD is perfect'[22] and that God 'does not change like shifting shadows'.[23] What is more, he is personal. He speaks, chooses, cares and gives. He also promises, 'Those who seek me find me.'[24]

Even of those who deny his existence, God says that the requirements of his law are 'written on their hearts'.[25] The conscience is God's fingerprint, an inescapable reminder of our moral obligation to obey him in everything. Whenever you pass judgement on your own behaviour, or on the behaviour of others, you are confirming that you are under the authority of a transcendent moral code. Even the modern atheist Richard Taylor is forced to this conclusion: 'The concept of moral obligation [is] unintelligible apart from the idea of God.'

The pretender

In 1999 Richard Dawkins told a BBC Television audience, 'I think science really has fulfilled the need that religion did in the past of explaining things: explaining why we are here, what is the origin of life, where did the world come from, what life is all about ... science has the answers.' Seeing science as the key to all reality and scientific investigation as the absolute and only way to get at the truth about anything is a line often taken by atheists and at a 1998 Oxford University debate Peter Atkins crystallized its conclusions: 'There is no necessity for God because science can explain everything.' *But true science makes no such claims*. Instead, it is the ongoing search for truth in the natural world, prepared not only to abandon previously held positions in the light of new discoveries but to admit that there are important areas in which science must remain silent.

To claim that all reality can be reduced to atoms and molecules and that a scientific explanation of things is the only true one is clearly at odds with the facts. The artistic description of a glorious sunset would differ widely from a scientific analysis of the same event, but it would be equally valid. To speak of a kiss as 'a juxtaposition of orbicular muscles, with a reciprocal exchange of carbon dioxide and microbes' would be scientifically accurate, but it is not the only acceptable description.

True science accepts that it has clear limitations. It cannot tell us why the world came into being (in other words, why there is something instead of nothing); or why dependable laws of physics exist; or why human beings are persons and not just what someone has called 'computers made of meat'; or why the mind exists and functions as it does; or how to distinguish between right and wrong. It also contradicts all four of Dawkins' claims: it does *not* tell us why we are here, how life originated, where the world came from and what life is all about. Answers to these questions are simply beyond the reach of scientific investigation.

The fact is that modern science owes much of its initial impetus to men who believed in creation as the work of God and the Bible as the Word of God. They studied science because they expected law in nature — and they expected law in nature because they believed in a divine lawmaker. In 1662 the founders of the Royal Society, the world's first major scientific institution, dedicated their work 'to the glory of God', while in 1865 the first manifesto of the British Association for the Advancement of Science

declared that the Bible was the Word of God and 'in complete harmony with the natural sciences'.

Over the centuries, many scientific giants have found no conflict between science and belief in God. These have included Robert Boyle (chemistry), Michael Faraday (electricity, electrochemistry and electromagnetism), James Joule (thermodynamics), James Clark Maxwell (electromagnetic theory and electrodynamics), Johannes Kepler (astronomy), Carolus Linnaeus (biological taxonomy), Blaise Pascal (hydrostatics), Niels Steno (stratigraphy), Gregor Mendel (genetics), Rudolph Virchow (pathology) and William Thomson (mathematics of heat and electricity). Today, countless fine scientists, including many of outstanding merit, are firmly convinced that the Bible is the Word of God.

True science and belief in God have always been in perfect harmony with each other. Trying to drive a wedge between them is ignorance masquerading as intelligence.

The attack

Another challenge argues that if God was all-powerful and all-loving, as the Bible claims, he would step in and prevent all evil and suffering. As these obviously exist, God must be powerless, loveless or non-existent. This sounds unanswerable — but is it?

Even without the Bible's specific teaching on the origin of sin and suffering (we will come to this later) there are logical hurdles to get over before we could buy into this 'package'. Atheism has no rational answer, while a powerless or loveless God would be a contradiction in terms, as by nature God is the very opposite of these. Can we sensibly hold a 'righteous God'[26] responsible for such things as our own deliberate dishonesty, selfishness, greed, immorality, cruelty, injustice and racial prejudice, or blame him when human error or carelessness leads to injury or death?

Yet God is not an impotent spectator when these things happen, not even when there are 'innocent victims'. The Bible says that although under no obligation to do so he often intervenes to prevent evil and suffering. As 'the Sovereign LORD'[27] he is in complete control even when sin is rampant and suffering at its worst. A survivor of Auschwitz, the Nazi extermination camp, said, 'It never occurred to me to … blame [God] or believe in him less, or cease believing in him at all.' Millions testify that God has used suffering to develop depth of character, deepen their concern for the needs of others and remind them of the brevity of life, the certainty of death and the eternal realities beyond the grave. Countless believers bear impressive witness that they can cope with great suffering through 'the strength God provides'.[28] Finally, in a way utterly beyond our understanding God will eventually bring about 'a new heaven and a new earth, the home of righteousness'[29] when the problem of evil and all its consequences will be fully, finally and perfectly settled beyond all doubt or dispute.

These things aside, the case against God has a fundamental — and fatal — flaw: in a universe without him how can we classify *anything* as 'good' or 'evil'? As we have seen, evolution provides no guidelines, nor does public consensus or personal opinion. Left to ourselves, we have no reliable reference point and are trapped in what someone has called 'that hopeless encounter between human questioning and the silence of the universe'.

But our creation by a holy God who gave us moral discernment would explain our conviction that there is a radical difference between right and wrong. Individual judgements may differ, but the very fact that we make them points *towards* the existence of God, not away from it.

What is more, disposing of God strips us of any sensible basis for empathy or sympathy. If we are merely uncreated 'stuff', what can we say to people traumatized as a result of natural disasters, accidents, disease or 'man's inhumanity to man'? When thirteen people died in a road accident near London in 1993 a leading British atheist said that in a world without God 'some people are going to get hurt, other people are going to get lucky, and you won't find any rhyme or reason in it'. Did that help those hurting or bereaved? When terrorists left 2,800 bodies buried under the rubble of New York's World Trade Centre in 2001, atheism could describe it as a violent redistribution of atoms and molecules, but could offer nothing by way of moral explanation. Can we seriously live with that and shrug off what happened as a meaningless event in a meaningless world? Far from disposing of God, our sense of good and evil suggests exactly the opposite.

25

In 1665 London was devastated by the Great Plague, which in a few months took the lives of 100,000 people. 318 years earlier a similar pandemic, gruesomely named the Black Death, swept across Europe, claiming over 20,000,000 victims, one third of the continent's population.

These and other massive outbreaks of bubonic plague are terrible pinnacles in human suffering, but they are mere pinpricks compared to one that struck thousands of years earlier and even now affects every person on the planet. The Bible's most concise statement about it says that 'sin entered the world through one man, and death through sin'.[30] This clinically summarizes the fact that although created by God 'in his own image'[31] and enjoying a perfect relationship with him in a flawless universe, our first parents wilfully chose to rebel against their Creator — with catastrophic consequences. These included the fact that their children, and their billions of successors since, were all born infected with the same deadly disease, one that pollutes the mind, the will, the affections, the imagination and the disposition, and leaves its victims exposed to God's holy anger.

There are no exceptions. Many people are in denial of the fact that they are sinners in God's sight, claiming that they live perfectly acceptable lives and only the most heinous behaviour would qualify them for that description; but the Bible shatters this illusion: 'If we claim to be without sin, we deceive ourselves and the truth is not in us.'[32] Like everybody else, the writer — and reader — of this sentence are people whose natural inclination is to rebel against God's 'good, pleasing and perfect will'.[33] Nor is our rebellion a minor offence against the majesty of God, for the 'most important [commandment]' is 'Love the Lord your God with all your heart and with all your soul and with all your mind and with all your strength'[34] and as we have not kept it we are all guilty of committing the greatest sin — and of doing so day after day.

There is no excuse. There are no reluctant rebels against God's will. We are sinners not merely by birth, but by choice. There is no man-made law that forces anyone to murder, rape, commit adultery, lie or steal; or to be proud, envious, greedy or vicious; or to be immoral in thought, word or deed. Instead, the Bible speaks of those who 'love evil rather than good'[35] and who 'delight in doing wrong'[36] even though their consciences point them to their Creator's transcendent law.

There is no escape. In 2001, scientists at The Sanger Centre, Cambridge, worked out the complete genetic structure of the bacilli responsible for bubonic plague. With bio-terrorism a contemporary threat, effective treatment for the disease is needed urgently. But there is no man-made cure for sin. Many turn to religion of one kind or another, but the Bible makes it crystal clear that nobody can get right with God by any kind of religious observance. Nor can sin be cleansed and conquered by moral resolution or determination. Turning over a new leaf does nothing to obliterate past sin and the Bible bluntly warns us that as counterweights to our godless thoughts, words and actions 'all our righteous acts are like filthy rags'.[37] None of them can wipe out our past record or make up for a lifetime of deliberate disobedience. Even believing the truth about God does nothing to change our sinful natures. Left to ourselves we are guilty, lost and helpless.

Casualties this Week.	
Imposthume	11
Infants	16
Killed by a fall from the Belfrey at Alhallows the Great	1
Kingsevil	2
Lethargy	1
Palsie	1
Plague	7165
Rickets	17

The exception

The scourge of sin has blighted all sixty billion people who have ever lived on our planet, with just one exception — Jesus of Nazareth, who was born in Israel about 2,000 years ago. The Bible clearly establishes three facts about him.

Firstly, his humanity. Jesus was not an android or any other kind of science-fiction freak, but was truly and fully human. Charting normal physical development, the Bible progressively describes him as a 'baby',[38] a 'child'[39] and a 'boy'.[40] He had to learn to stand, walk, write, feed and dress. His hair grew, his voice broke and he passed in the normal way through puberty into manhood. We read of him being 'hungry'[41] and 'thirsty'.[42] He called certain people his 'friends';[43] there were others he 'loved'.[44] He frequently 'had compassion'[45] on people as he identified with their pain. There were occasions when he 'wept'[46] over those heading for disaster, while he could also be 'full of joy'[47] as he delighted in the success of others. His humanity was beyond question.

Secondly, his integrity. Another clear mark of his humanity is seen in his being 'tempted in every way, just as we are'.[48] Yet in the same sentence we are told he was 'without sin'.[49] His enemies admitted it, his followers believed it, his closest friends noticed it and he himself claimed it. Speaking of Satan's power to plague people's lives, he added, 'He has no hold on me',[50] indicating that although under incessant spiritual attack he remained unscathed and unstained. Nobody else in history has been able to substantiate a similar claim. Jesus never felt guilty or ashamed; he never regretted anything he thought, said or did; he never needed to apologize or change his mind. The Bible's consistent testimony is that Jesus 'had no sin',[51] but was 'holy, blameless, pure, set apart from sinners'.[52]

Thirdly, his divinity. Although he was truly human, the Bible makes it clear that Jesus was just as truly divine. In one of its most concise statements on the subject it describes him as one 'in [whom] all the fulness of the Deity lives in bodily form'.[53] Jesus possessed not merely divine *attributes*, but the very *nature* of God, including his eternal existence. This means that although there was a day when Jesus was born, there was never a point at which he began to exist. He is *eternal*, without beginning or end, but his birth marked the moment when, as God, he began to live as a human being. Yet in doing so, he still remained fully God.

The Bible underlines this in the most emphatic way possible by attributing to Jesus actions that only God can perform. Speaking of Jesus it says, 'For by him all things were created: things in heaven and on earth, visible and invisible … all things were created by him and for him.'[54] What is more, it adds that 'in him all things hold together'.[55] Nature is not held in balance by chance, fate or unplanned laws of nature. What prevents our cosmos from becoming chaos is the sovereign power of Jesus of Nazareth, humankind's only true exception.

The mediator

Shortly before his death in 1996, Carl Sagan wrote, 'Our planet is a lonely speck in the great enveloping cosmic dark. In our obscurity, in all this vastness, there is no hint that help will come from elsewhere to save us from ourselves.' This was a powerful reflection of his worldview, but a poor response to the evidence.

We certainly need help, because sin (any deviation from God's perfect law) has left mankind morally degraded and spiritually destitute. We are able to break out of earth's gravity and reach the moon, but we are incapable of breaking free from our sinful bias and getting right with God. Not even a radical and permanent change in our behaviour would wipe out any guilty stains from our past, nor would it alter the fact that at heart we are 'deceitful above all things and beyond cure'.[56] The Bible's verdict is terse and terrible — we are 'without hope and without God in the world'.[57] If we are to be rescued from the penalty and power of sin, God must intervene on our behalf.

He did. The infinite gulf between a holy Creator and ourselves as flawed human beings could be bridged only by someone who was at one and the same time both God and man, and therefore able to meet the demands of one and the needs of the other. The previous section showed us that Jesus is precisely that person and the Bible confirms this by saying, 'There is one God and one mediator between God and men, the man Christ Jesus.'[58] Jesus did not come into the world as a politician, a financier, a psychologist or a doctor, because mankind's greatest need is not political, financial, mental or physical. Our greatest need is spiritual, to be delivered from the penalty and power of sin — and 'Christ Jesus came into the world to save sinners.'[59]

Jesus lived a perfect life, his teaching has never been equalled, and he performed countless miracles; yet these were indications of his identity rather than his prime purpose for coming into the world. In the words of his own mission statement, he came 'to seek and to save what was lost'[60] — to rescue men and women from the guilt and grip of sin and restore the broken relationship between God and man. His mission was accomplished not just by his life, but supremely by his death, when he took upon himself the guilt and condemnation that others deserved and suffered sin's appalling penalty in their place. His death was an amazing demonstration of God's perfect justice, which demands that every sin ever committed must be punished. To satisfy this demand, Jesus the sinless mediator chose to become accountable for the sins of others, just as if he himself had committed them. The Bible also tells us that in the death of Jesus 'God demonstrates his own love for us'.[61] In the person of Jesus, God took upon himself our human form and nature and bore in full the dreadful punishment his own justice decreed. *The Judge was judged in the place of others.* Nowhere in the Bible does the love of God for undeserving sinners shine more powerfully than in the death of Jesus.

Three days later, he was 'declared with power to be the Son of God, by his resurrection from the dead'.[62] His self-offering had been completely and dynamically vindicated.

The hinge

When I asked an atheist student at the University of Cape Town, 'What do you think of Jesus Christ?' he replied, 'I am not sure, but I do know this: everything hinges on whether he rose again from the dead.'

He was exactly right. If Jesus never rose from the dead, the New Testament has no more value than a handful of confetti, the first disciples were blasphemous deceivers, the early Christian church was a rabble of misguided bigots, all Christian martyrs have spilled their blood defending a non-event and the church's great reformers of society were motivated by a pack of lies. What is more, every Christian church building is a monument to a myth, all its ministers are liars, every prayer offered to or in the name of Jesus is pointless prattle, all who claim a living relationship with him are pathetically deceived, every Christian service is a farce, every Easter Day commemorates something that never happened and any hope of life after death is deluded daydreaming.

Some sceptics say that as miracles never happen the resurrection can be dismissed as nothing more than a religious fairy tale, but this argument is hopelessly illogical, as it assumes the conclusion before examining the facts. To believe that miracles never happen is as much an act of faith as to believe that they do, and rejecting them out of hand makes neither good science nor good sense. The right way to assess the validity of the resurrection of Jesus is to look at the evidence.

Many alternative theories have been put forward: 'Jesus never died'; 'The tomb was not empty'; 'The body was stolen'; 'The Roman authorities removed the body'; 'Jesus' followers removed it'. But these and other ideas have long ago and easily been exposed as hollow, while there are at least three powerful reasons for believing that the resurrection truly happened.

Firstly, the testimony of hundreds of eyewitnesses. The Bible says that within forty days of his resurrection Jesus appeared to well over five hundred people. The individual testimonies on record are completely consistent and defy all attempts to dismiss them as hallucinations. Sceptics had ample opportunity to interrogate the witnesses, yet there is not a single record of anyone retracting their claim that they had 'seen the Lord'.[63]

Secondly, the sudden transformation of the disciples. Before the resurrection they were traumatized and terrified, skulking behind locked doors. Their hero had been killed and as his followers their own lives were on the line. Yet suddenly they were transformed into a dynamic, heroic and fearless group of men, fully prepared to be imprisoned, tortured or executed rather than deny that they had met with the risen Jesus. Theoretically, they could have staked their lives on a falsehood they believed to be true, but it would have been psychologically impossible for them to do so by holding to something they knew to be false.

Thirdly, the existence and growth of the Christian church. It was not long before its enemies said it had 'turned the world upside down'[64] and today it is the largest religious movement in history. Yet its foundation is not a moral or ethical code, a certain stance on social issues or a particular religious ritual, but on one bedrock fact: *the resurrection of Jesus Christ.* It is obviously true that many are nominal members of the movement and as such add no credibility to the cause, but the revolutionized lives of millions more are dynamic testimonies to the truth of its foundation.

The needs

Towards the end of his life Bertrand Russell confessed, 'The centre of me is always and eternally a terrible pain — a curious wild pain — a searching for something beyond what the world contains.' Many today share Russell's frustration.

- There is the search for *truth*. Most people accept that all truth is relative and that something can be 'true for you but not for me'. Yet this defies common sense and would leave us with a world in which truth no longer had any value. The American author Neal Donald Walsch claimed, 'Feelings are your truth' — but what if others feel differently? Without what someone called 'true truth' no statement about anything has any value. In 2005 the British band Oasis released a best-selling album called *Don't believe the truth* — yet we *long* for truth we can trust. We are swamped with conflicting ideas and beliefs and are tired of subtlety and spin.

God is the answer. He is 'upright and just';[65] all his words are 'right and true; he is faithful in all he does'[66] and 'in him there is no darkness at all'.[67]

- There is the search for *identity*. Looking back on a brilliant career, the American film director Robert Altman reflected, 'If I had never lived, if the sperm that hit the egg had missed, it would have made no difference to anything.' Countless people feel the same isolation and emptiness. Realizing that none of their possessions, abilities and achievements can meet their deepest needs, they echo journalist Bernard Levin's haunting question, 'Have I time to discover why I was born before I die?'

God is the answer. Our true value lies not in our achievements or material possessions, but in who we are. Although sharing the same chemistry and biology as the animals, we are not jumped-up apes, nor are we a random cocktail of chemicals. We are spiritual beings, created 'in the image of God'.[68] Our rationality and moral sense are clear marks of this, but the greatest indication of our unique identity is our capacity to enjoy a living relationship with our Creator.

• There is the search for *love*. The American music group Black Eyed Peas hit the jackpot with their 2003 single 'Where is the love?', which exposed a world in which we are pressurized into believing that love without sex is nothing but a sentimental whim. In the last of the famous *Matrix* films Agent Smith summarized a central theme by saying that 'only a human mind could invent something as insipid as love'. Yet at heart we long for relationships that go beyond the physical and involve partnership, trust, respect, mutual commitment, self-giving and sacrifice.

God is the answer. One of the Bible's most stunning statements is 'God is love.'[69] It constantly reveals his passionate longing for a living relationship with people, one in which they are 'dearly loved'[70] and can become dynamically aware of his 'unfailing kindness',[71] 'great compassion'[72] and 'all-surpassing power'.[73]

• There is the search for *security*. We all have a longing to belong, to escape from the sense that we are orphans in a land of no tomorrow, moving relentlessly towards the moment when we are forced to part with all the things we cherish most.

God is the answer. Christians form a worldwide family in which each member is of equal worth and can serve a cause far greater than any other. Furthermore, that security extends beyond the grave, where God promises an eternal enjoyment of his presence and where there will be 'no more death or mourning or crying or pain'.[74]

The way in

The Canadian novelist Douglas Coupland, who hit the headlines with his 1991 novel *Generation X: Tales for an Accelerated Culture*, identified with those who rejected idealism and religion. Yet two years later he confessed, 'with the openness of heart that I doubt I shall ever achieve again ... My secret is that I need God.'

We all need God. Quite apart from leaving us with the needs we have just noted, our sin leaves us exposed to the appalling and eternal consequences that will follow the day of final judgement. This means that we need not only to know about God, *but to enter into a personal relationship with him* — and he wants this to happen. The sin-bearing death of Jesus in the place of those who openly choose to reject him demonstrates God's loving determination to rescue sinners and the resurrection of Jesus from the dead reveals that there is a 'new and living way'[75] by which we can enter his family and kingdom.

Responding to a living person is not like responding to a logical proposition. Getting right with God involves personal commitment, in which we 'turn to God in repentance and have faith in our Lord Jesus'.[76]

Simply put, *repentance* means that we must not only grieve over our godless words, thoughts and actions, but also have a genuine desire to turn from sin and to 'serve the living and true God'.[77] An Old Testament liar, adulterer and murderer got it absolutely right when he prayed, 'Create in me a clean heart, O God, and renew a right spirit within me';[78] so did a greedy New Testament extortionist who cried out, 'God, have mercy on me, a sinner.'[79]

Are you willing to follow their example? The Bible says that God 'commands all people everywhere to repent'[80] and will not forgive any sin that you are not willing to forsake. It also makes it clear that those who refuse to repent are utterly without excuse and 'suppress the truth by their wickedness'.[81] Are you willing to live a God-centred life instead of one that is self-centred? True repentance leaves no room for compromise.

The Bible's teaching about *faith* is equally clear. There is overwhelming evidence for the divine identity of Jesus, for his death in the place of others and his resurrection from the dead — and refusal to accept the evidence is an act of sinful defiance. Yet faith in Jesus goes beyond believing these things to be true. It means trusting completely in him as the 'one mediator between God and men',[82] who alone can heal the breach caused by our sin.

This entails abandoning your trust in everything else, including your sincerity, your respectability and any moral and spiritual merit you may feel you can claim. You must come to Jesus in true repentance, empty-handed, casting yourself on him alone to give you his priceless gift of forgiveness which will save you from the guilt and consequences of your sin. Writing about the nature of true faith, the German scientist and Nobel prize-winner Werner Heisenberg was absolutely right: 'If I have faith, it means that I have decided to do something and I am willing to stake my life on it.'

To all who are willing to make this wholehearted commitment, God makes the wonderful promise, 'You will seek me and find me when you seek me with all your heart.'[83] Millions of people all around the world, from every background and culture, would join me in testifying to the truth of these words — and you can do the same. Turn to him now, confess your need and cast yourself upon his mercy, his love, his grace and his power. Discover for yourself the dynamic reality of a personal relationship with Jesus Christ, who is 'the true God and eternal life'.[84]

Bible references

1. 1 Peter 1:23
2. Psalm 95:3
3. Psalm 90:2
4. John 4:24
5. Jeremiah 10:10
6. Deuteronomy 33:27
7. Psalm 33:11
8. Genesis 14:22
9. Psalm 103:19
10. Ephesians 1:11
11. Psalm 135:6
12. Exodus 15:11
13. Psalm 97:2
14. Psalm 118:1
15. Hebrews 4:13
16. Hebrews 9:27
17. Romans 14:12
18. Acts 17:31
19. Matthew 25:46
20. Genesis 1:1
21. 1 Chronicles 29:11
22. Psalm 19:7
23. James 1:17
24. Proverbs 8:17
25. Romans 2:15
26. Psalm 7:9
27. Ezekiel 14:6
28. 1 Peter 4:11
29. 2 Peter 3:13
30. Romans 5:12
31. Genesis 1:27
32. 1 John 1:8
33. Romans 12:2
34. Mark 12:29, 30
35. Psalm 52:3
36. Proverbs 2:14
37. Isaiah 64:6
38. Luke 2:16
39. Luke 2:40
40. Luke 2:43
41. Matthew 21:18
42. John 19:28
43. John 15:15
44. John 11:5
45. Matthew 9:36
46. Luke 19:41
47. Luke 10:21
48. Hebrews 4:15
49. Hebrews 4:15
50. John 14:30
51. 2 Corinthians 5:21
52. Hebrews 7:26
53. Colossians 2:9
54. Colossians 1:16
55. Colossians 1:17
56. Jeremiah 17:9
57. Ephesians 2:12
58. 1 Timothy 2:5
59. 1 Timothy 1:15
60. Luke 19:10
61. Romans 5:8
62. Romans 1:4
63. John 20:25
64. Acts 17:6, NKJV
65. Deuteronomy 32:4
66. Psalm 33:4
67. 1 John 1:5
68. Genesis 1:27
69. 1 John 4:16
70. Colossians 3:12
71. Psalm 18:50
72. Nehemiah 9:19
73. 2 Corinthians 4:7
74. Revelation 21:4
75. Hebrews 10:20
76. Acts 20:21
77. 1 Thessalonians 1:9
78. Psalm 51:10, ESV
79. Luke 18:13
80. Acts 17:30
81. Romans 1:18
82. 1 Timothy 2:5
83. Jeremiah 29:13
84. 1 John 5:20

If you have come to acknowledge Jesus Christ as your Saviour and Lord through the reading of this booklet, and would like help in beginning to read the Bible for yourself, you are invited to write to Dr John Blanchard, c/o Evangelical Press, Faverdale North, Darlington, DL3 0PH, England, for a free copy of *Read Mark Learn*, his book of guidelines for personal Bible study based on Mark's Gospel.

   If you need further help, please contact the following person:

For further reading

John Blanchard has written many books dealing in greater depth with the credibility, importance and relevance of the Christian faith and the following titles are among those currently available:

 Does God Believe in Atheists? This 658-page hardback traces the development of atheistic and agnostic thinking over the past 3,000 years, exposes the flaws in secular humanism and many world religions, and points the way to the true and living God. One reviewer called it 'crystal clear, devastating in its logic, compassionate at heart'.

 Has Science got rid of God? A 160-page paperback — reviewed as 'a must for the serious thinker' — that focuses directly on the title's question, explains the difference between science and scientism, examines the claims made on science's behalf, and shows why science and faith are allies not opponents.

 Is God past his Sell-by Date? In these 272 pages John Blanchard takes many of the issues raised in *Is anybody out there?* to another level. Reviewed as being 'readable, engaging and challenging', this book shows how we can know that God is real, relevant and accessible.

 Where is God when things go wrong? These 40 pages show why we can trust God even when we cannot trace him. 'Clear, powerful, timely and important', it explains why evil and suffering do nothing to disprove the existence of an all-powerful, all-loving God.

All of the above are available from the publisher:

Evangelical Press, Faverdale North, Darlington, DL3 OPH, England
e-mail: sales@evangelicalpress.org

Evangelical Press USA, PO Box 825, Webster, New York 14580, USA
e-mail: usa.sales@evangelicalpress.org

web: http://www.evangelicalpress.org